Computer

Excel Magic

Claire Pye and Paul Virr

W
FRANKLIN WATTS
LONDON·SYDNEY

Paperback edition first published in 2004
Franklin Watts
96 Leonard Street
London EC2A 4XD

Franklin Watts Australia
45-51 Huntley Street
Alexandria
NSW 2015

© Franklin Watts 2003

Created by:
act-two
346 Old Street
London EC1V 9RB
www.act-two.com

Text: Paul Virr
Consultant: John Siraj-Blatchford
Managing editor: Claire Pye
Editor: Deborah Kespert
Designers: Ariadne Boyle, Tim Clear
Illustrators: Ian Cunliffe, Andrew Peters
Art director: Belinda Webster
Editorial director: Jane Wilsher

A CIP catalogue record for this book
is available from the British Library.

ISBN 0 7496 5860 6 (pbk)

Printed in Hong Kong, China

Contents

Words marked in **bold** in the
text are explained on page 32.

How to use this book
Look at the pictures in this book
to find out what's happening on
your computer screen.

Follow each numbered step in
the book and on your computer.

> **1** Double-click
> on Microsoft Excel.

Coloured arrows show
you where to look on
your computer screen.

Words that are
underlined tell you
what to do next.

Introducing Excel

In this book, you'll find out how to record information in a **computer program** called Microsoft Excel. Then, you'll use Excel to show your information in all kinds of ways, from colourful tables to **column charts** and **pie charts**.

Let's investigate

One way of collecting information is to carry out a survey. We carried out a survey about hair colour. We asked all the pupils in Class 1 and Class 2 what colour hair they had. Then, we entered the results into a table in Excel.

A survey can tell you lots of interesting things! Try one out on your friends, your family or the rest of your class.

Multi-coloured Hair Survey					
Hair colour	Brown	Blond	Black	Ginger	Total
Class 1	10	5	3	2	20
Class 2	6	8	4	0	18

Column chart

You can use Excel to change information into a column chart. Look at the chart below. Can you see that 4 pupils in Class 2 have black hair?

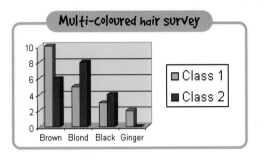

Multi-coloured hair survey

Pie chart

In Excel, you can also change information into a clever pie chart like the one below. We'll show you how to make a pie chart later on.

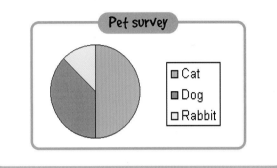

Pet survey

Mouse magic

When you move your mouse, a shape, called a **cursor**, moves around the screen. In this book, you'll need to move your cursor and click with your mouse. Here are the different ways of clicking.

Double-click
Press the left button twice, quickly.

Drag
Press the left button and move the mouse at the same time.

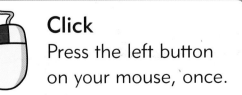

Click
Press the left button on your mouse, once.

Explore Excel

It's time for you to open Excel and
learn how to find your way around!

1 First, find
Microsoft Excel
and double-click
on it to open it.

2 This is an
Excel **spreadsheet**.
It's like a big table
that's made up of
columns and rows.

3 A column runs
from top to bottom.
It starts with a letter.

4 A row runs
from left to right. It
starts with a number.

5 Each little box in this spreadsheet is called a cell. The black line around the cell shows you that it is **selected**. Here, cell A1 is selected, which means you're working in this cell.

6 To select a different cell, just click on it. <u>Click on cell C5 now.</u> C5 is the cell where column C meets row 5.

7 You can also look in this box to find out which cell is selected.

Let's play 'Find a Cell'! One person calls out the letter and number of a cell, and the others see who can click on it first. Have a go!

Enter information

Now you can move from cell to cell, you're ready to start typing in Excel!

1 We're going to type in the results of the hair colour survey from page 4. First, click on cell A1 to **select** it.

Microsoft Excel - Book1

File Edit View Insert Format Tools Data Window Help

Arial   10   B *I* U   ≡ ≡ ≡   % ,

A1   =

	A	B	C	D	E	F
1						
2						
3						

3 When you have finished typing, press the Enter key on your keyboard. Now cell A2 is selected.

2 Use your keyboard to type in the name of your survey.

Microsoft Excel - Book1

File Edit View Insert Format Tools Data Window Help

Arial   10   B *I* U   ≡ ≡ ≡   % ,   .0 .00   100%   ?

A2   =

	A	B	C	D	E	F	G	H	I
1	Hair Survey								
2									

4 If you make a mistake, you can easily change it. First, select cell A1 again by clicking on it.

5 Now type in your new title and press your Enter key.

Microsoft Excel - Book1

File Edit View Insert Format Tools Data Window

Arial ▾ 10 ▾ **B** *I* U ≡ ≡

	A	B	C	D
1	Hair Survey			
2				
3				
4				
5				

Microsoft Excel - Book1

File Edit View Insert Format Tools Data Windo

Arial ▾ 10 ▾ **B** *I* U ≡ ≡

✗ ✓ = Multi-coloured Hair S

	A	B	C	D
1	Multi-coloured Hair Survey			
2				
3				
4				
5				

Practise your typing by copying the rest of the information from the survey. Remember to click on a different cell each time you type.

Microsoft Excel - Book1

File Edit View Insert Format Tools Data Window Help

Arial ▾ 10 ▾ **B** *I* U ≡ ≡ ≡ ⊞ 🔄 % ,

E5 ▾ =

	A	B	C	D	E	F
1	Multi-coloured Hair Survey					
2	Hair colour	Brown	Blond	Black	Ginger	Total
3	Class 1	10	5	3	2	
4	Class 2	6	8	4	0	
5						
6						
7						
8						
9						
10						
11						

Save your work

Let's give this Excel **spreadsheet** a name and save it in the My Documents **folder**.

It's important to save your work. If you don't, the next time you switch off your computer, it will be lost forever!

Microsoft Excel - Book1

Insert Format Tools Data Window Help

100%

	A	B	C	D	E	F	G	H	I
1	Multi-colour Hair Survey								
2	Hair colour	Brown	Blond	Black	Ginger	Total			
3	Class 1	10	5	3	2				
4	Class 2	6	8	4	0				
5									

Sheet1 / Sheet2 / Sheet3 /

Ready

NUM

1 Find this Save button and click on it.

2 In the Save As box, you can choose a folder to store your work. Let's store this spreadsheet in the My Documents folder. Click on this button.

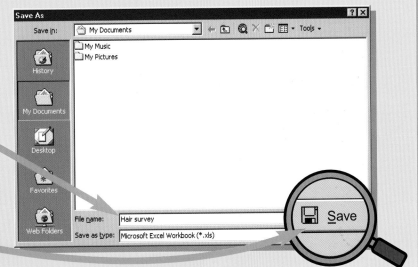

3 Now choose a new name for your spreadsheet! Use your keyboard to type it in.

4 Click the Save button.

5 Can you see the name you typed? It's up at the top of your spreadsheet.

Save As

Save in: My Documents

History

My Documents

Desktop

Favorites

Web Folders

My Music
My Pictures

File name: Book1.xls

Save as type: Microsoft Excel Workbook (*.xls)

Save

Cancel

Save As

Save in: My Documents

History

My Documents

Desktop

Favorites

Web Folders

My Music
My Pictures

File name: Hair survey

Save as type: Microsoft Excel Workbook (*.xls)

Save

Microsoft Excel - Hair survey.xls

File Edit View Insert Format Tools Data Window Help

Arial   10 **B** *I* <u>U</u>

E4   =

	Multi-coloured Hair Survey				
1	Hair colour	Brown	Blond	Black	Ginger	Total
2	Class 1	10	5	3	2	
3	Class 2	6	8	4	0	
4						
5						
6						

Add it up!

Here's a great trick for adding
up numbers the easy way!

1 Let's add up the number of pupils in Class 1 and enter the total in cell F3. Click on cell F3.

2 Now find this Autosum button and click on it.

Microsoft Excel - Hair survey.xls

File Edit View Insert Format Tools Data Window

Arial   10   B I U

F3   =

	A	B	C	D	E	F	G	H	I
1	Multi-coloured Hair Survey								
2	Hair colour	Brown	Blond	Black	Ginger	To			
3	Class 1	10	5	3	2				
4	Class 2	6	8	4	0				
5									
6									
7									
8									
9									
10									
11									
12									
13									
14									
15									
16									
17									

3 This dotted line shows us the cells that Excel is going to add up for us.

4 Press your Enter key to make the answer appear!

5 Ta-da! As if by magic, the total number of pupils in Class 1 appears in cell F3!

Microsoft Excel - Hair survey.xls

File Edit View Insert Format Tools Data Window Help

AVERAGE = =SUM(B3:E3)

	A	B	C	D	E	F		H
1	Multi-coloured Hair Survey							
2	Hair colour	Brown	Blond	Black	Ginger	Total		
3	Class 1	10	5	3	2	=SUM(B3:E3)		
4	Class 2	6	8	4	0			
5								
6								

Hey presto!

Arrows away!
You can also move around Excel using the arrow keys on your keyboard. Why not give it a try?

Microsoft Excel - Hair survey.xls

File Edit View Insert Format Tools Data Window Help

Arial 10 B I U 100%

F4 =

	A	B	C	D	E	F	G	H	I
1	Multi-coloured Hair Survey								
2	Hair colour	Brown	Blond	Black	Ginger	Total			
3	Class 1	10	5	3	2	20			
4	Class 2	6	8	4	0				
5									

Sheet1 Sheet2 Sheet

Ready   NUM

Now try some more maths magic. Can you add up the number of children in Class 2? Enter the answer in cell F4.

13

Decorate your table

Make your table multi-coloured
with a few wizard tricks!

1 Click in cell A1. Then, keep your mouse
button held down and drag the **curso**r to cell F4.
Have you **selected** all the cells in your survey?

	Microsoft Excel - Hair survey.xls								

File Edit View Insert Format Tools Data Window Help

Arial 10 B I U % Multi-coloured Hair Survey

A1 = Multi-coloured Hair Survey

	A	B	C	D	E	F	G	H	I
1	Multi-coloured Hair Survey								
2	Hair colour	Brown	Blond	Black	Ginger	Total			
3	Class 1	10	5	3	2	20			
4	Class 2	6	8	4	0	18			

2 Click on Format.

3 Next, click on Autoformat.

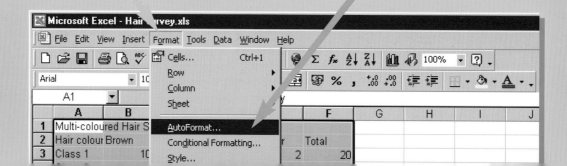

Microsoft Excel - Hair survey.xls

File Edit View Insert Format Tools Data Window Help

Arial 10

A1

	A	B
1	Multi-coloured Hair S	
2	Hair colour	Brown
3	Class 1	10

Cells... Ctrl+1
Row
Column
Sheet

AutoFormat...
Conditional Formatting...
Style...

Total
20

4 Choose a style for your table. We've chosen Classic 2. Click on Classic 2.

5 Click on the OK button.

AutoFormat ? ✕

	Jan	Feb	Mar	Total
East	7	7	5	19
West	6	4	7	17
South	8	7	9	24
Total	21	18	21	60

Simple

	Jan	Feb	Mar	Total
East	7	7	5	19
West	6	4	7	17
South	8	7	9	24
Total	21	18	21	60

Classic 1

	Jan	Feb	Mar	Total
East	7	7	5	19
West	6	4	7	17
South	8	7	9	24
Total	21	18	21	60

Classic 2

	Jan	Feb	Mar	Total
East	7	7	5	19
West	6	4	7	17
South	8	7	9	24
Total	21	18	21	60

Classic 3

	Jan	Feb	Mar	Total
East £	7 £	7 £	5 £	19
West	6	4	7	17
South	8	7	9	24
Total £	21 £	18 £	21 £	60

Accounting 1

	Jan	Feb	Mar	Total
East £	7 £	7 £	5 £	19
West	6	4	7	17
South	8	7	9	24
Total £	21 £	18 £	21 £	60

Accounting 2

OK
Cancel
Options...

6 Finally, click anywhere to see your colourful and stylish table!

Microsoft Excel - Hair survey.xls

File Edit View Insert Format Tools Data Window Help

Arial 10 B I U % , 100%

H1 =

	A	B	C	D	E	F	G	H	I
1	**Multi-coloured Hair Survey**								
2	**Hair colour**	Brown	Blond	Black	Ginger	Total			
3	**Class 1**	10	5	3	2	20			
4	**Class 2**	6	8	4	0	18			
5									
6									

Add some colour

Make your table look a treat by adding a bright splash of colour.

	A	B	C	D	E	F	G
1	Multi-coloured Hair Survey						
2	Hair colour	Brown	Blond	Black	Ginger	Total	
3	Class 1	10	5	3	2	20	
4	Class 2	6	8	4	0	18	
5							

Microsoft Excel - Hair survey.xls

File Edit View Insert Format Tools Data Window Help

Arial 10 B I U

B3 = 10

1 Let's **select** the numbers in our **spreadsheet**. Click in cell B3 and drag to cell F4.

2 Find this Fill Colour button. Click the small arrow next to it.

3 Choose the colour you want and click on it.

No Fill

4 Click anywhere to see the results of your decorating!

I've chosen green, my favourite colour. Why don't you try out some different colours to see which you like best?

Microsoft Excel - Hair survey.xls

File Edit View Insert Format Tools Data Window Help

Arial   10   B I U

G6   =

	A	B	C	D	E	F	G	H	I
1	Multi-coloured Hair Survey								
2	Hair colour	Brown	Blond	Black	Ginger	Total			
3	Class 1	10	5	3	2	20			
4	Class 2	6	8	4	0	18			
5									
6									
7									
8									
9									
10									
11									
12									
13									
14									
15									
16									
17									
18									
19									
20									
21									

Sheet1 Sheet2 Sheet3

Ready   NUM

Column Charts

Create a colourful **column chart** to bring your survey to life!

	A	B	C	D	E	F	G	H
	Microsoft Excel - Hair survey.xls							
	A2		= Hair colour					
1	**Multi-coloured Hair Survey**							
2	**Hair colour**	Brown	Blond	Black	Ginger	**Total**		
3	**Class 1**	10	5	3	2	20		
4	**Class 2**	6	8	4	0	18		
5								

1 **Select** part of your table. Click on cell A2, then drag to cell E4. Be careful not to select the Total column.

2 Next, find this Chart Wizard button and click on it.

18

Chart Wizard - Step 1 of 4 - Chart Type

Standard Types | Custom Types

Chart type:
- Column
- Bar
- Line
- Pie
- XY (Scatter)
- Area
- Doughnut
- Radar
- Surface
- Bubble
- Stock

Chart sub-type:

Clustered column with a 3-D visual effect.

Press and Hold to View Sample

Cancel | < Back | Next > | Finish

3 We're going make a column chart. Make sure the word 'Column' is selected.

4 Now click on a style for your chart. We've chosen a 3-D style.

5 Finally, click on the Finish button to see your chart magically appear!

Microsoft Excel - Hair survey.xls

File Edit View Insert Format Tools Data Window Help

Arial | 10 | B I U

H4 | =

	A	B	C	D	E	F	G	H
1	Multi-coloured Hair Survey							
2	Hair colour	Brown	Blond	Black	Ginger	Total		
3	Class 1	10	5	3	2	20		
4	Class 2	6	8	4	0	18		
5								
6								
7								
8								
9								
10								
11								
12								
13								
14								
15								
16								
17								
18								

Chart showing Brown, Blond, Black, Ginger for Class 1 and Class 2.

Hey presto!

Move it!
You can move your chart around by clicking on it and dragging it with your mouse. Try to find the perfect position for it on your spreadsheet.

Colourful columns!

Change the colours of your columns to create a super stylish chart!

1 Let's brighten up this chart! <u>First, double-click on the grey background.</u>

Microsoft Excel - Hair survey.xls

File Edit View Insert Format Tools Data Window Help

Arial 10 **B** *I* <u>U</u> 100%

H4 =

	A	B	C	D	E	F
1	Multi-coloured Hair Survey					
2	Hair colour	Brown	Blond	Black	Ginger	**Total**
3	Class 1	10	5	3	2	20
4	Class 2	6	8	4	0	18

□ Class 1
■ Class 2

Brown Blond Black Ginger

Sheet1 Sheet2 Sheet3

Ready NUM

2 Now pick a new colour and click on it. We've chosen green.

Hey presto!
Column colours
You can change the colour of the columns on your chart, too! Just double-click on a column. Then pick a new colour and click OK.

Format Walls   ? ✕

Patterns

Border
- ○ Automatic
- ○ None
- ● Custom

Style: �_____▼

Color: �_____▼

Weight: �_____▼

Area
- ○ Automatic
- ○ None

Fill Effects...

Sample

OK   Cancel

3 Finally, click on OK to add a splash of paint!

Microsoft Excel - Hair survey.xls

File Edit View Insert Format Tools Data Window Help

Arial   ▾ 10 ▾ B I U ≡ ≡ ≡ ▦ 💲 % , ⁺⁰ ·⁰⁰ ⁙ ⁙ ▦

H4   =

	A	B	C	D	E	F	G	H
1	Multi-coloured Hair Survey							
2	Hair colour	Brown	Blond	Black	Ginger	Total		
3	Class 1	10	5	3	2	20		
4	Class 2	6	8	4	0	18		
5								

I've changed some more colours on my chart. Can you make your chart look like mine?

21

Pie Charts

Let's carry out a new survey about pets and turn the results into a **pie chart**.

We asked our friends which pets they owned. Then, we followed the steps in this book to record the results. Can you make your survey look like ours?

Microsoft Excel - Pet Survey.xls

File Edit View Insert Format Tools Data Window Help

Arial   9   **B** *I* U

B2   = Cat

	A	B	C	D
1	Pet Survey			
2	Pet	Cat	Dog	Rabbit
3	Number	8	6	2

1 You need to **select** the information in your **spreadsheet**. Click on cell B2 and then drag to D3.

2 Next, find the Chart Wizard button and click on it.

3 Choose a new type of chart, here. Click on Pie.

4 Now click on the Finish button.

5 As if by magic, a pie chart appears! The biggest slice of pie is for cats, which shows that cats are the most popular pet.

Chart Wizard - Step 1 of 4 - Chart Type   ? X

Standard Types | Custom Types

Chart type:
- Column
- Bar
- Line
- Pie
- XY (Scatter)
- Area
- Doughnut
- Radar
- Surface
- Bubble
- Stock

Chart sub-type:

Pie. Displays the contribution of each value to a total.

Press and Hold to View Sample

Cancel   < Back   Next >   Finish

You've cooked up a tasty pie chart! Now follow the steps on pages 10-11 to save your pet survey.

Microsoft Excel - Pet Survey.xls

File Edit View Insert Format Tools Data Window Help

Arial   10   B I U

F1   =

	A	B	C	D	E	F	G
1	Pet Survey						
2	Pet	Cat	Dog	Rabbit			
3	Number	8	6	2			
4							

- Cat
- Dog
- Rabbit

23

More colour tricks

Some bright and fruity colours will make the slices of your **pie chart** look even more scrumptious!

1 First, click on the pie chart to **select** it.

2 Next, choose just one slice by clicking on it.

3 Double-click on the slice you've selected.

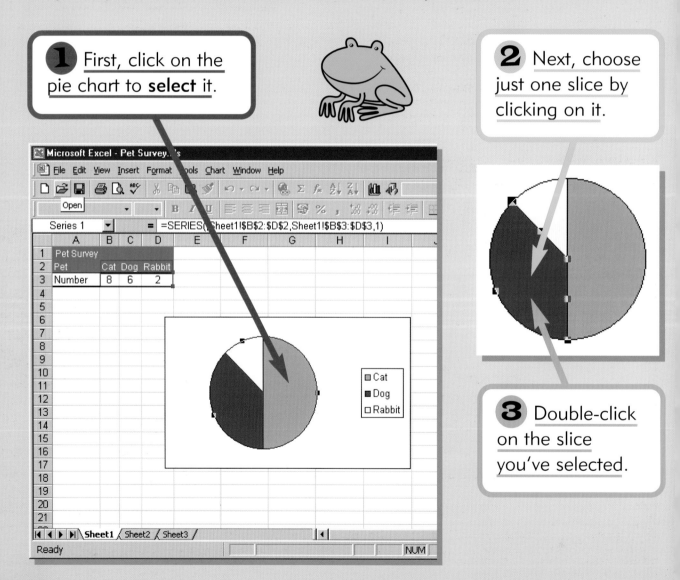

Format Data Point

Patterns | Data Labels | Options

Border
- ● Automatic
- ○ None
- ○ Custom

Style: _____
Color: Automatic
Weight: _____

☐ Shadow

Sample

Area
- ○ Automatic
- ○ None

Fill Effects...

OK   Cancel

4 Now choose a colour and click on it. We've chosen the colour orange.

5 Finally, click the OK button.

We've changed more colours in our pie chart. Can you do the same?

Microsoft Excel - Pet Survey.xls

File Edit View Insert Format Tools Data Window Help

Arial   ▼ 10 ▼ **B** *I* U ≡ ≡ ≡ ▦ ⑨ % , ⁺.₀ .₀₀ ⁞⁞

K2   =

	A	B	C	D	E	F	G	H	I
1	Pet Survey								
2	Pet	Cat	Dog	Rabbit					
3	Number	8	6	2					
4									
5									
6									
7									
8									
9									
10									
11								□ Cat	
12								■ Dog	
13								□ Rabbit	
14									
15									
16									
17									
18									
19									
20									
21									

Sheet1 / Sheet2 / Sheet3 /

Ready   NUM

25

Printing time!

It's time to print out your **spreadsheet** so you can display it on the wall!

1 To see how great your spreadsheet will look when it's printed out, <u>click this Print Preview button</u>.

2 Print Preview shows you how your table and chart will look when they're printed out. If you're ready to print, click the Print button.

3 Click on the OK button to print out your spreadsheet.

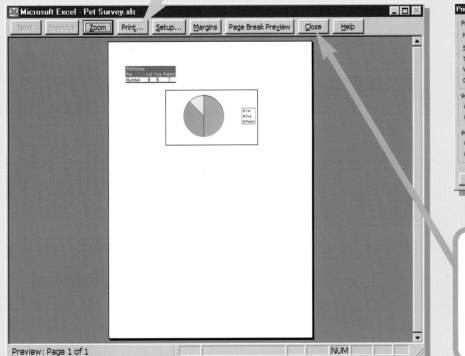

4 If you want to make more changes, click the Close button to close Print Preview.

Why not print out more copies for your friends?

find your work

Find out how to close down Excel, and how to find your **spreadsheets** again later.

1 When you've finished working and want to stop, remember to save with a click on the Save button.

2 To close Excel, find the Close button in the top corner and click on it.

3 Now, let's track down your spreadsheets! You saved them in the My Documents **folder**, so double-click on My Documents to open it up.

Microsoft **Windows**98

My Documents

Network Neighborhood

Recycle Bin

Start 16:00

4 My Documents opens, with your spreadsheets inside! Double-click on the one you want to open.

You're a spreadsheet wizard! Now, why not carry out a survey about your friends' favourite cartoon characters or how much TV they watch?

My Documents

File   Edit   View   Go   Favorites   Help

Back   Forward   Up   Cut   Copy   Paste   Undo   Delete   Properties   Views

Address   My Documents

My Music   My Pictures   Hair survey.xls   Pet Survey.xls

My Documents

Select an item to view its description.

27.6KB   My Computer

Guidance notes

In this book, children get to grips with surveys, tables and charts with the help of a spreadsheet program called Microsoft Excel.

Microsoft Excel

Microsoft Excel is part of the Microsoft Office suite of programs. This book is compatible with Microsoft Office '97, 2000 and XP, although there may be slight variations between versions.

Macintosh users

Macintosh computers with Microsoft Excel Macintosh Edition can be used with this book. Please note that mouse clicks work differently with Macintosh computers and some buttons and toolbars may look different.

How to set up your computer

Children will find it easier to follow the steps if you set up your computer to look like the one in the book. Here's how.

Your desktop

Some computers may not have an Excel shortcut on the desktop. Here's how to create one.
❶ Click Start, open Programs and find Excel.
❷ Right-click on the Excel shortcut and drag it to a blank space on your desktop.
❸ Select 'Create shortcut here' from the menu.

Excel Toolbars

Now open Microsoft Excel and make sure the following toolbars are open.
❶ Right-click on a blank area of the grey toolbars at the top of Excel.
❷ Make sure that only the following toolbars are ticked: Standard and Formatting.

Save your work

Encourage children to save their work often. It's good practice to save work in My Documents so that it's easy to find later. However, if you are working from a network with a group of children, you may need to set up individually named folders and show them how to find them in the Save As dialog box.

Extension activities

Each chapter of Excel Magic is self-contained so children can learn at their own pace. Hey presto! boxes contain tips and ideas for extra practice. Below and on the following page, there are more extension activities.

Fun with surveys

Children can copy our survey or carry out their own on almost any subject, such as their favourite pop stars, sports or food.

Fun with tables

Ask children questions about the information in the table on pages 9-13. How many children in Class 2 have blond hair? Use Excel to add up other totals in the table, such as the total number of pupils with brown hair in both classes.

Fun with charts

Ask children questions about the charts in the book. According to the column chart on page 19, how many children in Class 2 have ginger hair? According to the pie chart on page 23, which pet is the least popular?

Experiment and enjoy!

Encourage children to experiment with different chart types on pages 19 and 23 and then discuss which types are more or less effective. Then, they can add colour and display their charts on the wall.

Make it fun!

Ask children about what they are doing and invite them to think about what they are going to do next. Encourage and praise them as they learn, and remember not to cover too much at once!

Health and safety

Supervise children when turning the computer on and off. Remind them not to put their fingers inside the computer at any time. Encourage them to take regular breaks to avoid repetitive strain injuries and eyestrain. Refer to the computer manual for information about the correct seating and posture. Children should be sitting upright with their feet on the floor and the keyboard in line with their elbows.

National Curriculum links for Information and Communication Technology

Key stage 1

Finding things out
- ✔ 1a. Gathering information from a variety of sources.
- ✔ 1b. Entering and storing information in a variety of forms.
- ✔ 1c. Retrieving information that has been stored.

Developing ideas and making things happen
- ✔ 2a. Using text and tables.

Exchanging and sharing information
- ✔ 3a. Sharing ideas by presenting information in a variety of forms.

Key stage 2

Finding things out
- ✔ 1c. Interpreting information.

Developing ideas and making things happen
- ✔ 2c. Using simulations and exploring models to answer 'What if...?' questions.

Exchanging and sharing information
- ✔ 3a. Sharing and exchanging information in a variety of forms.

Scottish National Guidelines 5-14 ICT

Strands covered at levels A and B
- ✔ Using the technology
- ✔ Collecting and analysing

Useful words

column chart

A column chart shows information in columns. To read a column chart, look at the height of a column against the number at the side.

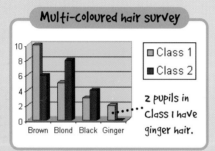

Multi-coloured hair survey

□ Class 1
■ Class 2

2 pupils in Class 1 have ginger hair.

Brown Blond Black Ginger

computer program

A computer program helps you to do different jobs on your computer. In this book, we use a program called Microsoft Excel to make tables and charts.

cursor

The cursor is the shape that moves on screen when you move your mouse. You use it to point to different parts of your screen.

This cursor appears when you point at buttons.

This cursor appears when you point at cells.

folder

A computer folder is used for storing work, just like a real folder. In this book, you store your work in a folder called My Documents.

My Documents

pie chart

In a pie chart, each coloured slice of pie stands for one part of the total.

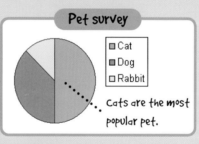

Pet survey

□ Cat
■ Dog
□ Rabbit

Cats are the most popular pet.

select

Select is another word for 'choose'. In Excel, you click on a cell to select it. A selected cell has a thick black line around it.

spreadsheet

A spreadsheet program looks like a big table with columns and rows. You use a spreadsheet to record information, add up numbers and make charts.

Index